WELSH VALLEYS
PHRASEBOOK

GET BY IN VALLEYS-SPEAK

D0755098

About *Welsh Valleys Humour*, by the same author

Ronnie Barker

What a delight David Jandrell's book is.
He, like me, loves words, and finds them
irresistibly funny. I hope you will too.
I know you will. Take my word for it.

Readers' comments

Welsh Valleys Humour made me laugh…
and laugh… and laugh! Yes – Wales
(our bit, anyway) really is like that.

Hilarious and VERY true little book
of the Valleys' humour! Well worth buying
and highly recommended!

WELSH VALLEYS PHRASEBOOK

GET BY IN VALLEYS-SPEAK!

David Jandrell

BSc BA(Hons) PcET Cert Ed.

y Lolfa

First impression: 2017
© David Jandrell & Y Lolfa Cyf., 2017

Cover design and illustrations: Siôn Jones

ISBN: 978 1 78461 405 8

Published and printed in Wales
on paper from well-maintained forests by
Y Lolfa Cyf., Talybont, Ceredigion SY24 5HE
e-mail ylolfa@ylolfa.com
website www.ylolfa.com
tel 01970 832 304
fax 832 782

Contents

dedicated to:

Roy, Joan, Rose, Malcolm, Breeze, Norman, Blinz, Roxy, Gutser, Jack the Hat, Bonnie, Clyde, Sam, Horace, Boris, Doris, Rabies, Pebbles, Tilley, Rex, Sweepy and Nesbitt.

How to use this book

Unlike most books, this one begins with a set of guidelines. Lightweight instructions, if you like. This doesn't mean that when you've finished it you'll be able to fix your car or install a washing machine, because it isn't an instruction manual per se. The guidelines are merely to help you to follow the way that the book's set out and, hopefully, to embrace its full purpose.

If you're a person who wants to learn Welsh, this book is not for you.

If you're a person whose first language is Welsh and you want to improve your spoken English, this book is not for you.

If, on the other hand, you're an English speaker who's due to visit the Welsh Valleys – maybe on holiday, going to a wedding, or simply travelling through Wales and you know at some stage you're going to need to stop for a toilet break or a meal – this book is definitely for you.

A first visitor to the Valleys will almost certainly have to converse with a local at some stage, and that's where the trouble may start. Ask for directions and you'll be no better off than if you'd bought a sat nav and the speaker gave all directions in Klingon. You'll have very little idea of what's been said to you. You'll probably assume that the person you spoke to answered you in Welsh. The reality is that the person will actually have been speaking to you in English – and it's this version of English that this book's all about: the non-standard English used in the Valleys in everyday conversation, also known as Valleys-speak, or Wenglish. This language is far removed from the English that you'll be used to, and hopefully these pages will ease your communication problems during your time in the area.

Although, at first glance, you may wonder what language it's written in, it's actually written in English. The phonetic version of the spoken language, that is. Pronunciation is the biggest hurdle to overcome, and this book was prepared with that in mind. The thing to remember here is that our non-standard words are not necessarily pronounced the Welsh way, even though those words may look like Welsh on paper! So, if you see an English word, say it as that word's pronounced in English. That will be how it's pronounced in Wales – the difference being that the word will mean something else. See *oven* in the Phrasebook section (p.77) as an example.

The Phrasebook will define the most common anomalies you'll come across, and the following guidelines should take you through pronunciation at an appropriate level to enable you to communicate as an equal throughout the Valleys.

Compulsory Terms

You'll find some ongoing themes which may not be included in the Phrasebook section in any great detail. This is because they're so common and will probably form the bulk of all conversations you have. These are your 'bread and butter' words and phrases, if you like, and I thought it would be expedient to address those here so that you have a good grounding before we reach the Phrasebook, where the real fun starts. But, in the meantime, let's start off with these darlings…

Aitch or *Haitch?*

The letter 'H' is never, repeat NEVER, sounded where it should be in standard Valleys community-based conversations. The 'H' sound can be heard, however, in two situations. The first is when the speaker's actually spelling out the letter 'H'. Here the 'H' sound will be very prominent, even protracted, to inform the listener that it's very important to not drop aitches, especially when using the word 'aitch' itself.

Example:

'Your surname please?'

'Jones.'

'And your initials?'

'D. H. That's deeee… **hhhhhhhaitch**.'

'Er… thank you, Mr Jones.'

The second is when the speaker's trying to sound posh, either face to face or by adopting a posh 'phone voice' when speaking to someone whom they deem to be posher, of higher authority or superior to themselves. This practice is pretty hit and miss, will normally contain more 'H' sounds than the conversation needs and they will, most certainly, be sounded in the wrong places.

Example:
"Ello Mr (H)Evans. (H)I'm phonin' to see (H)if you can pop round my 'ouse later to 'ave a look at my gas cooker. The rings won't light and the (H)oven door won't (H)open tidy.'

I was in a quandary when I compiled the 'H' section in the Phrasebook because I realised that we don't use it, so how could I include it in a Phrasebook arranged alphabetically? I did include some instances, but on the whole in the examples that accompany definitions, you'll see several 'H' words appear in a phonetic format: an apostrophe followed by the rest of the word.

hand → 'and
horse → 'orse
head → 'ead, etc.

The same 'rule' applies to words that begin with a 'wh' spelling but the 'H' sound. In this case, as before, words like 'who' and 'whom' will become *oo* and *oom*.

-ng
The 'ng' sound at the end of words is, again, very rarely sounded. Instead, we prefer to shorten the sound to a plain, common-or-garden 'n'. As in:

shortenin'
abridgin'
clippin'
abbreviatin', etc.

Taking this one stage further, below I've selected an 'H' word which ends with an 'ng' sound to show you how it will appear in the Phrasebook and examples. The word I've selected for this demonstration is the standard English word, 'howling'. For our purposes, this becomes *'owlin'*. Here are a few more for your delectation: *'untin'*, *'elpin'*, *'angin'*, *'eavin'*, *'avin'*, *'aberdasherin'*, etc.

The *En* Verb

The next thing to grasp is the much-used verb, *en* or *ent*.

If you're over a certain age, cast your mind back to your school grammar lessons and your introduction to verb study. I can remember it now: ah yes, the old verb 'to be', which we learned by rote. There was even a little tune to go with it. So we sang a little song which complemented the lyrics below.

Here's a reminder:

I am	We are
You are	You are
He/She/It is	They are

Woe betide anyone who said 'I are' or 'they am' in the individual questioning session after the 'to be' song. Interestingly, in the Valleys the use of *they am* is actively encouraged and heard all the time. This is an anomaly in its own right and, along with its *butties* (friends), is explored in depth below.

Back to *en* and *ent*. Effectively, this is a study of the verb 'to not be' and would fit the 'to be' tune perfectly. In fact, in the corridor and in the playground our song became the *en* and *ent* song – after we'd made sure we were out of earshot of our teachers, of course. They were still administering the cane in those days, you know.

We don't really bother with grammar in the Valleys. All this 'I' and 'am' business! Far too much to remember. No, we just say *en* or *ent* to everything, as in the familiar pattern below:

I en(t)	We en(t)
You en(t)	You en(t)
He/She/It en(t)	They en(t)

'What's the difference between *en* and *ent*?', I hear you ask. In truth, there's no difference per se. If you were to hold a gun to my head to pressurise me into coming up with a difference, I would have to say that *ent* tends to be used in more formal situations. Perhaps if one was speaking to someone in

ARE YOU THE OWNER OF THIS VEHICLE, SIR?

NO, I ENT. AND I OVEN 'AD A DRINK NEITHER.

authority, or maybe just wanting to sound forceful, then *ent* would possibly be deemed to be more appropriate.

Example:
'Mr Lewis, I believe this is the fourth time you've been before me in this court.'
'No, it **ent,** your honour – fifth or sixth, maybe, but definitely more than four.'

They Am

As promised, we now move on to *they am* – in fact in Wales, we shorten it to *theym*. Here, we adopted the first person singular 'am' and decided to use it for most of the rest too. So our song template for this case would become:

I'm
Youm

Heez/Sheez (NB not 'Heem/Sheem')
Weem
Youm
Theym

Example:
'**Weem** goin' down the pub later. **Weem** meetin' Bob and Carol there.'
'**Youm** meetin' Bob and Carol?'
'Aye.'
'Well, if **theym** gonna be there, we en goin'.'
Why's that, then?'
'We en keen on Bob and Carol. **Weem** uneasy in their company.'

Do do

This is probably my favourite. We in the Valleys don't do something, we do do it. So, if you ask someone what they do for a living, they'll have to say, in full:

'I do do bricklayin'.'
'I do do nursin'.'
'I do do firefightin'.', etc.

Needless to say, we don't normally go the whole hog and say the phrase in its full form, we shorten the first 'do' to just the consonant sound 'd' so that the audible response to the above question becomes:

'I d'do fishin'.'

Similarly:

'I d'go....'
'I d'be...'
'I d'love...', etc.

Ironically, the English have a perfectly acceptable phrase which is the negative version of 'I do do', and that's 'I don't do.'

'Do you do drugs in England?'
'No, we don't do drugs in England.'

Odd, I think, that 'I don't do' sounds perfectly normal, but when we say 'I do do', people run around in utter confusion trying to decipher what these mad Welsh people have just said to them.

I've tried to think of a good example of this trait and I can't better the example given in *Welsh Valleys Humour* (by my good self), so here it is again. I was once called upon to 'translate' a phrase that had been used by a fluent 'Valleys speaker'. The person who needed my assistance was a Cardiff boy, who was totally unaware of Valleys-speak and had no concept of the grammar and syntax associated with it.

He had asked the advice of a Valleys speaker on how to grow runner beans, and had listened intently to all the instructions and the methods used for a successful crop. He admitted that he had understood most of the instructions, but had been totally floored by the concluding sentence. The sentence that had caused the confusion was '…and if you d'do what I d'do and you d'do it right, you'll be right. Right?'

This came perfectly naturally to me, but the Cardiff boy stated that if the runner bean king had summed up the instructions in French, his level of misunderstanding couldn't have been any greater. At the time I was a little sad when I realised that the two men had resided no more than 18 miles apart all their lives, and this total lack of knowledge of Valleys-speak existed to such an extent that I had to act as an interpreter!

If I'd thought of it at the time, I would like to have explained what the runner bean expert had said by saying, 'What he meant was that if you d'do what he d'do and you d'do it right, you'll be right. Right?' It would have been funny, I suppose, but it always seems to be the case that you can think of something better to say when the moment's gone.

The Dreaded *W*

One day, a friend who was English (still is, actually) was making his way from 'across the bridge' to visit me when he got lost. He rang me to see if I could give him directions, and of course I needed to ask him where he was. He replied, 'Well,

I don't know. I've just gone through this village. I don't know what it's called because on the map the name's about six inches long and it contains no bloody vowels!'

It did actually. He didn't realise that we have seven vowels this side of the bridge. These are:

A   E   I   O   U   W   Y

We slipped a couple of sneaky ones in at the end.

It's the sounding of the 'W' vowel sound that I want to deal with here.

Our 'W' vowel sound is depicted as ʊ in dictionaries and other guides to pronunciation. ʊ? Any the wiser? No? Nor me.

So we'll forget the academic stuff and use my method. Much easier. Think of the English word 'soot'. Our 'W' vowel sound sounds like the way that the 'oo' is sounded in 'soot', or the way that the 'u' is sounded in the northern English pronunciation of 'pub' or 'duck'. So that's what ʊ is!

In the following Phrasebook and examples, to differentiate between the ʊ-sounding 'W' vowel and words that contain a conventional English 'W' consonant sound (as in 'wish'), I have underlined the 'W' which should give the ʊ vowel sound, e.g. c_wtch, _wnt, d_wnt, _wman, etc.

T and Th

We're also a bit shy when it comes to sounding 't' and 'th' sounds.

As with Cockney English, this is quite apparent when a 't' sound comes at the end of a word. The Cockneys, however, tend to end these words abruptly, using a technique known as a glottal stop. We, on the other hand, like to drag out the vowels preceding the final 't' until they fade away into the distance.

Here's a phrase that will lose its 'th' and 't' sounds:

What's that?   → *Waaassssaaaaaa.......?*

Similarly, and perhaps an oddity at the same time, is the phrase 'like that', as used when someone's showing someone else how to do something. It nearly follows the 'rule' but there is a slight difference. The 'th' and 't' sounds disappear as expected, but for some reason, the 'k' in 'like' also morphs into a 'g' sound. So:

Like that. → *Lie-gaaaa.*

So, try to follow a brief conversation showcasing this anomaly. To start you off, the first speaker says, 'What's that you're doing?'

'Waaassssaaaaaa youm doin'?'
'Fixin' my tyre.'
'Why are you doin' it lie-gaaaa?'
'I've always done it lie-gisssssss!'
'I d'do it lie-gisssssss, lie-gisssssss and finish it off lie-gisssssss. Job done.'
'Show me again?'
'Lie-gisssssss, lie-gisssssss and finish it off lie-gisssssss.'
'So it's lie-gaaa, lie-gaaa and finish it off lie-gaaaa?'
'Exactly lie-gaaa, butt.'
'Tidy, I won't do it lie-gisssssss any more, I'll do it lie-gaaaa from now on, like you d'do it.'

Spot on or nearby?

If you ask a Welsh person where they are, where something is, where they've been, or where they're going, you may not be much the wiser after the answer you get. We tend to like to retain a bit of mystery as to the whereabouts of the object of enquiry by not pinpointing its exact location, but steering you towards somewhere nearby. A form of guessing game if you like, played and enjoyed by all.

I mean, of course, the habit of saying *by here* or *by there*.

So if you ask where the *Radio Times* is and the response is 'By there', you may well be in the same boat as you were before you asked the question. The responder will be making some gesture, either with their eyes or pointing with a finger, which means that you must make a conscious effort to observe them when they respond so that you can follow the physical signs to find what you're looking for.

On the other hand, the responder may be more specific and reply with a 'By there by the coffee table.' This will enhance your chances of success at finding the *Radio Times* exponentially because all you then have to do is find the coffee table and hunt around in that vicinity. The *by* in this case is actually a nondescript preposition of place. The *Radio Times* could actually be on the coffee table, on the floor at the side of the coffee table, a yard away from the coffee table or roughly within the same postcode that the coffee table's sitting in at the time. Quite a lot of scope there, but all perfectly acceptable.

You'll see that I did not exaggerate when I made reference to 'within the same postcode' when I tell you about a snippet I gleaned from an overheard conversation a few years ago:

'Where to is Manchester?'
'It's up north somewhere, up by Liverpool.'

In this case, the *by* represented a distance in the region of 34 miles! As you can see, in this case, it's actually exceeded the postcode boundary.

Asking and replying using the *by* method

There are no standard protocols when questioning and answering here. There are certainly no rules covering tense, grammar, syntax – this is entirely governed by the speaker, and depending on the speaker, this can become as convoluted as they deem appropriate. Here are some examples of questions/answers, which show the scope for the progression of bizarreness.

Questions	Answers
'Where to is it?	'It's up by yer.'
'Where is it to?'	'It's down under by there.'
'Where's it by?'	'It's over by there.'
'Where to is it by?'	'I don't know where to it's by.'
'Where by is it to?'	'It's up over by yer.'
'Where by will you be to?'	'In the bus station, by Burger King.'

To recap, where the hell is it anyway?

The Rogue *Ah*

I worked for a number of years in an area which came under the Rhondda Cynon Taff authority, and the Rogue *Ah* had completely passed me by until that time. To be fair, I was then bombarded with it on a daily basis for the following 13 years!

This is the penchant to tag an *ah* sound on to words that naturally end with an English 'Y' sound. So if you hear a kid in the street shouting, 'Mammyah, Mammyah,' he will actually be calling his mother ('Mammy, Mammy!'). This can be very off-putting when you hear it for the first time, and if used when giving directions, it can herald disasters of Olympic proportions.

Example:
'Well, where youm goin' is at the top of the valley**ah**. So, go down the A470**ah**, but not as far as Ponty**ah**, turn left by the pub called the Merry**ah** Miller, and it'll be down by there.'
'Thank you, what's your name?'
'Julie-**ah**'
'Thank you, Julia, for all your help.'
'No, my name's Julie-**ah**.'
'That's what I said.'
'No, you didn't, you said Julia – my name is Julie-**ah**.', etc.

Make statement, confirm statement, then question what you've just said

This is another acquisition from the Rhondda Cynon Taff area. It actually threw me completely when I heard it first, but, as in the case of the Rogue *Ah*, I got used to it.

I had greeted a new class and was getting to know the students. When I asked a particular lad what he did in his spare time, he said, 'I d'play rugby I do, don't I?'

Looking at that in detail:

I d'play (statement made)
I do (statement confirmed)
don't I? (questioning everything that's been said so far)

It turned out that most of the lads in the class played rugby they did, didn't they?

Example:

"Ow are you, Bob? 'Ow are you, Terry?'

'Alright, Bryn?'

'Wha' did you do on Friday?'

'We went to the club **we did, didn't we**?'

'Went together **you did, did you**, Terry?'

'Aye, Bob come with me **he did, didn't he**?'

'Wha' was it like?'

'It was alright **it was, wasn't it**?'

'Aye, until I got chucked out.'

'You got chucked out **you did, did you**?'

'Aye, got pissed **I did, didn't I**, so they chucked me out **they did, didn't they**?'

Reading the examples

When you're reading the Phrasebook, a brief example of the way each word is used in context accompanies each definition. The subject of the entry will be in **bold text**. The examples are likely to contain other words that are listed in the Phrasebook, and these will be in *italics* – should you need to refer to them to help make sense of the whole thing.

Here's an example of an example:

weem

We are.

> **Example:**
> '**Weem** *gwyin*' to Cardiff shoppin' *Satdee*.'
> 'Oh, **weem** *gwyin*' to Newport.'
> 'Fancy comin' to Cardiff with us instead?
> 'No, **weem** meetin' my sister in Newport *afta*.'

And now…

The Phrasebook

A

Aber-c<u>w</u>m-sc<u>w</u>t

(regional variations: **Aber-c<u>w</u>m-bucket** or **Aber-c<u>w</u>m-flopflop**)

Somewhere nondescript in Wales. Where people end up when they get lost.

Example:
'Well, we followed the directions to Cardiff to the letter and we ended up in **Aber-c<u>w</u>m-sc<u>w</u>t**.'

'*Ew* must 'ave gone wrong somewhere.'

'Definitely, *butt*.'

afta

1. Have to. 2. Later.

Example:
'*Ew*'ll **afta** come down and let me in, love. I lost my keys.'

'I might come down **afta** if *youm* lucky. Maybe that'll teach *ew* to look after 'em in future.'

alright or wha'?

Are you OK?

Example:
'What *arrew* doin' on the floor *butt*? 'Ave *ew* fell? *Ew* **alright or wha'**?'

'I'm alright – *jest* pissed, *thaaaa*'s all.'

'Oh, no need to fret then. See ya.'

'Aye, see ya.'

...and proud of it

Annoying, seemingly obligatory 'tag-on' phrase. Used mainly when someone says 'I'm Welsh ...**and proud of it**.'

Annoying? Yes, because as the speaker deems it necessary to add what appears to be a justification for uttering something controversial, they're suggesting that perhaps one shouldn't be seen to be proud of being Welsh. On the annoyance scale, it's up there with the phrase, 'for my sins,' which is tagged onto phrases in the same way, as in, 'I support Cardiff City... for my sins.' It's OK to say, 'I'm Welsh,' guys. That's all you need to say.

apparce

Half past (time measurement).

> **Example:**
> 'Wha' time's *ewer* appointment at the dentist?'
> '**Apparce** two.'
> '*Thaaaa*'s a good time to go to the dentist.'
> 'Eh?'
> 'Two thirty. "Tooth hurty." Geddit?'
> 'Oh, shut up, *ew* dozy *twonk*!'

arrew

Are you?

> **Example:**
> 'Where **arrew** off, *butt*?'
> 'Down the welfare to watch the Rangers.'

'Alright, **arrew**?'
'*Woddya* mean?'
'*Theym* terrible.'
'I've watched 'em for *yers*. Used to it now, *mun*.'

ast

Asked.

Example:
'*Ew gwyin*' to the pub tonight?'
'No, I *ent*.'
'Why not?'
''Cos *ew*'ll be there.'
'Wish I 'adn't **ast** now.'

avenue

Haven't you?

Example:
'**Avenue** got up yet?'
'No, I'm just thinkin' about it now.'
'Well, look sharp and get peelin' some spuds for tea.'

avew/uvew

Have you?

Example:
'**Avew** *bin* Christmas shoppin' yet? I done all mine in two hours.'
'**Uvew**? Blinkin' 'eck!'

B

bailey

An area at the front or rear of the house. Back yard.

> **Example:**
> 'Bob was a bit pissed last night I *yerd*.'
> 'He was too. I chucked the drunken slob out the **bailey** to sober up. '
> 'Where to is he by now?'
> 'Still out there, as far as I know.'

bamp/bampi

Affectionate term for one's grandfather. Also **granch**.

> **Example:**
> 'I've just seen *ewer* **granch**.'
> 'Were to was he by?'
> 'Down the OAP 'all with my **bamp**.'

bard

Ill, infirm, not well.

bardness

A word describing how *bard* someone is. There are three levels of **bardness**:

1. **Bard:** Head cold, off colour, migraine. Worth ringing into work for a day off.

2. **Awful bard:** At least a week off!

3. **Terrible bard:** Terminal. Well, at least in the eye of the sufferer!

> **Example:**
> "Ello, is the foreman there?'
> 'Yes, shall I get 'im?'
> 'No, *jest* tell 'im I phoned in **bard** so I <u>wnt</u> be in.'
> 'If he asks, 'ow **bard** *arrew*?'
> **'Terrible bard.'**

basterin'

An expletive, possibly a derivative of 'bastarding', although that word doesn't exist either. Used where 'bastarding' would be, if it was a word. Or it could be a slightly more polite alternative to 'f*cking' (when used to express contempt).

> **Example:**
> 'I went to the bar for a pint and it was **basterin'** *shut tap*. He <u>wdn</u> **basterin'** serve me. The **basterin'** bastard!'

bell-oil

Used to describe a loud cacophonous racket.

> **Example:**
> 'I've 'ad a gutsful of that cockatiel squawkin' all the time.'
> '*Bin* noisy today, 'as he?'
> 'Noisy? He've *bin* givin' it **bell-oil** all day!'

belong to ew

Be yours, in the parental sense.

Example:
'Oi, *thaaaa* boy with the Swansea shirt on. Do he **belong to ew**?'
'Aye. Why?
'He just smashed our window and when I shouted at 'im, he gimme a load of cheek.'
'*Woddya speckt* me to do about it?'

big massive

Huge. Opposite of **tiny lickle**.

Example:
'We was down the club earlier and this couple came in, and *ew shouldda* seen 'em. She was a **big massive** *bomper* and he was a *tiny lickle dwt*.'

bim

Generic name for an acquaintance. Similar to mate, buddy etc.

Example:
'Hiya **bim**, 'ow's it *gwyin*'?'
'Not so bad *mwsh* – 'ow's ewerself?'

bin

Been.

Example:
'Where've *ew* **bin**?'
'I *oven* **bin** nowhere.'
'I called round earlier and *ew* never answered the door.'
'Must've **bin** out the *gwli* puttin' the bin out.'
'Bin day today, *is it*?'

'Aye – *ew've* forgot, *avenue*?'
'Every week, *butt*. Fancy givin' me an 'and fly tippin' *afta*?'
'Aye, no problem, *butt*.'

bitter

Very cold, freezing.

Example:
'If *youm gwyin'* down the club, *ew* wanna put *summut* warmer than *thaaaa* on. It's blinkin' **bitter** out.'

blemmer

Usually a reference to a high level of skill involved in a sporting event. See **brahmer**.

boggin'

Unattractive, ugly, unappealing,etc. Similarly, regional variations: **bulin'**, **gompin'**, **mingin'**, **mulin'**, **muntin'**, **scruntin'**.

Example:
"Ave *ew* seen the state of Ron's new girlfriend? **Boggin'**, *mun*.'
'I *yerd* she was **bulin'**. *Thaaaa* bad, is she?'
'Oh aye, **gompin'**.'
"Is last girlfriend was no oil paintin', mind.'
'More like an oil slick – **mingin'** she was.'
'Oh aye, **mulin'**, *mun*.'
'Mind *ew*, *heez* **muntin'** – can't *speckt* 'im to pull any lookers, to be honest.'
'Aye, to be fair all 'is girlfriends 'ave *bin* **scruntin'**.'

boilt

Boiled.

> **Example:**
> 'The kettle 'ave **boilt** – make me a cuppa, I'm *starvin'*.'

bollockin'

Churn something out very quickly.

> **Example:**
> 'I went to the baker's and they'd sold out of them pasties by
> *apparce* nine this mornin'.'
> 'I *en* surprised. *Theym* bloody lovely, they are.'
> 'Makin' a fortune as well. They *en* 'alf **bollockin'** 'em out lately.'

bomper

Unusually large, oversized person.

> **Example:**
> 'Cor, flippin 'eck, I've just seen the new prop *oove* signed for the
> rugby club. *Heez* blinkin' 'uge, *mun*.'
> 'A proper **bomper**, is he?'

borrow

Lend.

> **Example:**
> 'Can *ew* **borrow** me a fiver till tomorrow?'
> 'On one condition.'
> *Wossat*?'
> '*Ew* gimme a tenner back.'
> '*Youm* a *kokum* sod *ew* are, aren't *ew*?'

bosh

Kitchen sink.

Example:
'Why *oven ew* done the washin' up?'
'*Ew* didn't tell me to do it.'
'I shouldn't 'ave to, *ew* can see there's washin' up to be done.'
''Ow am I supposed to know *thaaaa*?'
'*Jest* look in the **bosh**, love, it's full of dirty dishes!'

brack

A flaw or tear in fabric.

Example:
'I can't understand why *ew* keep wearin' that jumper. There's a 'uge **brack** right down the front of it.'

brahmer/blemmer

Usually a reference to a high level of skill involved in a sporting event, **brahmer** being very good, **blemmer** being very, very, very good.

Example:
'I *oven* seen the game yet but I *yerd* the first try was a blinkin' **brahmer**.'
'It was, but watch out for the fourth try 'cos that was an absolute **blemmer**.'
'I'll *afta* make sure I watch the replay on "Scrum 5".'

breckfusses

Plural of breakfast.

Example:
'We'd better get *summut* solid inside us before we d'start *swillin'*, boys. Stop the bus by *yer*, *Drive* – I'll go in thaaaa *caff* and order us 53 **breckfusses** with extra black puddin'.'

Bryn

Generic 'affectionate' name for a mate, pal or friend. See **butt**, **mwsh**, **bim**. Thought to originate in the Swansea area, but now sweeping across Wales. Could be a reference to the character in the film 'Twin Town'.

Example:
'Alright, **Bryn**?'
'Hiya, *butt*. 'Ow's it *gwyin'*, **Bryn**?'
'I'm alright, **Bryn**, aye.'

buffy

Buffet.

Example:
'*Arrew* comin' to our weddin' party in the night?'
'*Dunnow*, wha' time's the **buffy** on?'
'*Apparce* nine.'
'I'll see *ew* about *apparce* nine then, but I _wnt_ be stoppin' long.'

bulin'

Unattractive, ugly, unappealing, etc. See **boggin'**.

bung

Throw, chuck.

Example:
'Where to *arrew* off to?'
'I'm off out the kitchen to put the kettle on.'
'Do us a favour, **bung** us my fags over on *ewer* way out.'
'Where by are they to?'
'On the table by the kitchen door.'

bust/busted

Break/broke/broken.

Example:
'That toilet seat's **bust** again.'
'*Oove* **busted** it this time?'
'*Dunnow* but *theym* a dab 'and at **bustin'** it – *thaaaa*'s the third time in as many weeks.'

bute

Beaut. Affectionate term for a close friend or lover.

Example:
'Alright, **bute**? 'Ow's it *gwyin*?'
'Not bad, **bute** – 'ow's *ewer*self?'

butt/butty

Informal term of affection to a mate, pal, friend, associate. Probably the Welsh version of the American 'bud' or 'buddy'.

Example:
'Where to *arrew* off to, **butt**?'
'Alright, **butt**? I'm off to meet Bob down the park.'
''Ang on, **butt**, *yer*'s a stroke of luck – *yer* he comes. Alright, **butt**, 'ow's it *gwyin*?'

'Aye, I'm alright, **butt**. What about *ew*?'
'Alright, **butt**, aye.'
'*Tidy*.'

buzzin'

Smelly, whiffy.

Example:
'I went round my sister's 'ouse yesterday. *Sheez* got seven cats livin' there. It was absolutely **buzzin'** in there it was.'

bwgi

1. Buggy – home-made go-cart. See **gambo**.
2. Bogey – snot, booger, nostril detritus.

Example:
'Where's *our* Dai?'
'Down the park with 'is **bwgi**.'
'Which one? The one he rides on or the one stuck to the front of 'is shirt?'
'Both of 'em.'

bwgi ghost/bwgi-man

Menacing mythical creature used by adults to frighten children into good behaviour.

Example:
'If *ew* d'keep *mwchin'*, the **bwgi-man** will come and drag *ew* to school by *ewer* balls.'

C

cack

1. Faeces, poo. 2. To defecate, to poo. Also **pwp**.

> **Example:**
> 'That's the last time I take laxatives followed by a hefty pinch of snuff.'
> 'Sneezed and **cacked** *ewer* pants, did *ew*?'
> 'Oh aye, I should say so.'

cack-handed

Completely devoid of manual dexterity. An 'unhandyman'. Also **coggy-handed**.

> **Example:**
> '*Oo* the 'ell put them shelves up?'
> 'Me.'
> 'They *en* straight, *mun*!'
> 'I know, I'm **cack-handed**.'

caff

Café.

> **Example:**
> 'Just got chucked out of the **caff**.'
> 'Why?'
> 'Punchin' the *diddler*.'
> 'Nicked *ewer* money again, did it?'
> 'Aye.'
> 'Wha's their problem in there?'

cant

1. Gossip, rumour. 2. To gossip, rumour-monger, tittle-tattle.

Example:
"Ave *ew* seen Brenda? Can't find 'er nowhere.'
'She'll be down the road **cantin'**, I *speckt*. She never does *nowt* else, *chopsy* cow!'

carnew

Can't you?

Example:
'**Carnew** come to the club tomorrow?'
'Can't *butt*, I'm in court again.'
'**Carnew** give it a miss?
'*Gorroo mun*, or they'll bang me up again.'

carry clecks

1. A tell-tale tit, nark, informer. 2. To tell tales, grass up.

Example:
'Watch what *ew* do in front of 'er, mind.'
'Why's *thaaaa*?'
'*Sheez* **carryin' clecks** to the boss all the time, *mun*.'

catch my 'and

Hold onto me.

Example:
'Them vodkas 'ave went straight to my 'ead. I *onny* 'ad a couple.'
'**Catch my 'and**, love – I'll see *ew* 'ome safe.'

chairs

Cheers/Thank you. Creeping into retail/bar staff vocabulary recently. Users like to pronounce 'cheers' as **chairs**, possibly in a vain attempt to sound a bit posh and not in the slightest way pretentious or hollow.

> **Example:**
> 'I'd like to pay for my papers. Oh, and take for a bottle of milk as well, please.'
> '**Chairs**.'

chappin' my wick

Annoying me.

> **Example:**
> 'I 'ad to introduce Jason to the back of my 'and this afternoon.'
> 'Why's that, then?'
> 'He was **chappin' my wick** all mornin', and I'd 'ad a gutsful of it by this afternoon.'

cheekin'

Being cheeky.

> **Example:**
> 'I 'ate them next door's kids.'
> 'Why's *thaaaa*?'
> 'Full of *mwci nic* the lot of 'em, and **cheekin'** me when I d'tell 'em off.'

chimly

Chimney.

Example:

'If *ew d<u>w</u>n* behave *ewer*selves, when Father Christmas d'come down the **chimly**, he *<u>wnt</u>* be leavin' any presents for *ew* this *yer*.'

chopsin'

Speaking loudly, being precocious, verbally aggressive or gossipy. See **chopsy**.

chopsy

Loud, precocious, verbally aggressive, gossipy.

Example:

'It was supposed to be a silent vigil, but all *ew* could *yer* was 'er *chopsin'*.'

'Oh I know, *sheez* a bloody **chopsy** cow, 'er.'

...or

'*D<u>w</u>n* say anythin' in front of 'im if *ew d<u>w</u>n* want it broadcast all over the town, mind.'

'Oh I know, *heez* bloody **chopsy**, 'im.'

...or

'I *wozn g<u>w</u>yin'* to make an issue of it, but she came in and all 'ell broke loose!'

'Oh I know, *sheez* a bloody **chopsy** cow 'er.'

'*Sheez* got a bell on every tooth, that one.'

click

Exclusive group, clique. Also **clicky** (adjective form).

Example:

'I *bin gwyin'* down *thaaaa* club for ten *yers* and I still feel like a
    stranger in there.'

'Bloody **clicky** lot in there, *butt*. Always *bin* the same.'

cowin'

A mild expletive. An alternative to using 'something stronger'.

Example:

'I've 'ad a **cowin'** gutsful of them *basterin'* **cowin'** kids muckin'
about in the *gwli* all day. One of these days I'm *gwyin'* to get the
cowin' police *twum*!'

craxy

Irritable, touchy, short tempered.

Example:

'I *dunnow* wha's wrong with my son. I can't do anythin' right.
Heez stampin' around the 'ouse, shoutin' at the dog, throwin'
things around. Proper **craxy** he is today!'

cut any sway

Make a difference.

Example:

'Well, I bought my missus flowers and chocolates to get in 'er
    good books, but it didn't **cut any sway**.'

'She still got 'ay fever and diabetes?'

'Aye. Oh, *pwp*!'

SHE AST ME IF HER BUM DO LOOK BIG IN THEM JEANS. DUNNO WHAT MADE HER SO CRAXY.

cwmander

Commander as in 'TV remote control'. Also **remort**.

Example:
'I think the batteries is dead in this **cwmander**.'
'*Youm gwyin*' to *afta* get up off *ewer* arse and turn the telly over by pressin' the buttons on it then.'
'And I thought slavery 'ad *bin* abolished in this country!'
'It 'ave, but it's still *gwyin*' in this 'ouse.'
'*Dwn* I know it.'

cwpi down

Squat, crouch, cower. Also **twtti down**.

Example:
'Me and Violet got caught short on the way 'ome from the club.

Bustin' for a *wazz* we was, both of us. There was no bogs around so we 'ad to **cwpi down** in the back lane by the chip shop and do it by there.'

cwtch

A very common Welsh word, now understood by most English speakers. Made even more famous when Nigel Owens belittled brawling rugby players on national TV by saying, 'If you want a **cwtch**, do it off the field, not on it.'

Commonly, **cwtch** has three meanings:

1. A cuddle. Physical show of affection. 2. To hide something. 3. A place where you put things (like English 'cubby hole').

Example:
'I was wrappin' 'is birthday present and he walked in. I 'ad to
   cwtch it a bit quick under the cushion.'
'**Cwtch** it in the **cwtch**, then give us a **cwtch**.'

D

Dai (the)…

Contrived 'affectionate' name for a Welsh person (male or female) where a word for an occupation or a characteristic/trait is tagged onto **Dai** (the Welsh equivalent of 'Dave'), describing what that person does for a living or the way they're perceived.

Examples:
(NB all genuine cases)
Dai Pigs: Farmer (actually a sheep farmer – no pigs on his farm).
   Real name: David

Dai the Milk: Milkman. Real name: Howard

Dai Dog: Miner. Reason for nickname unknown – he didn't have a dog. Real name: Phil.

Dai Knick-Knacks: Female vocalist. Her underwear was visible through her clothing when on stage. Real name: Rachel

Dai Twenty-One: Unemployed. Not even Dai Twenty-One could remember how the name was initiated. Real name: David

Dai Foid Fever: Admin worker. Started in the sixties when schoolkids were inoculated against Typhoid Fever. Real name: David

Dai Skusstin: Teacher. Pupils coined this name when he stopped the class and told them that their language was disgusting. Real name: David

Dai the Bread: Baker. Real name: Ian

Dai Book and Pencil: Traffic Warden. Real name: unknown. Apparently even his wife referred to him as this.

Dai Mad: Female factory worker. Reputed to be a bit crazy. Real name: Kim

Dai Chip: Carpenter. Real name: Tony

Dai Eighteen Months: Had half an ear missing. Nickname originated when someone pointed out he had a 'ear and a half.' Honest! Real name: Bob

Dai Synth: Synthesiser operator and guitarist in late 70s band, Rudy and the Russians. Real name: David Jandrell (me!)

Dai Twice

Contrived name allocated to anyone whose real name is David Davies.

daps

Sports shoes, trainers.

Example:

'*Thaaaa* boy in orange **daps** playin' on the wing was a bit quick, wasn't he?'

'Nobody could catch 'im. Like Billy Whizz on speed, *butt*.'

dee

Day. This version is only found when pronouncing the days of the week.

Examples:

Mun**dee**

Tues**dee**

Wens**dee**

Thurs**dee** or Furs**dee** (interchangeable)

Fri**dee**

Sat**dee**

Sun**dee**

yester**dee**

diarrhoea with daps on

Very fast. Also **a fart with daps on**.

Example:

'Some bloody idiot kicked a ball up against our kitchen window and *bust* it!'

'Did *ew* catch 'im?'

'Nah, I ran out but he was gone like **diarrhoea with daps on**.'

diddler

Fruit machine, one-arm bandit, gambling device found in pubs and cafés.

Example:

'They 'ad a new **diddler** in the *caff* this mornin'.'

'*Woddya* mean 'ad? *En* it there no more?'

'Aye, its still there, but it's *bust*.'

''Ow did it get *bust*?'

'I *busted* it 'cos it wasn't payin' out.'

'*Dwn* blame *ew*, *butt*.'

do-ins

See **dooberry**.

dooberry

Generic name for something or someone used when the speaker either doesn't know the name of the subject, or can't be bothered to use it. Similarly: **do-ins**, **doodah**, **mackonky**, **oojackapivvy**, **shmongah**, **usser**, **whatewmcallit**, **woddewcall**, **wossnim**, etc.

Example:

''Ave *ew* seen the **dooberry**?'

'It's over by there by the **oojackapivvy**.'

'*Oo* put it there?'

'**Wossnim**, before he went into town.'

'*Wossee* gone to town for?'

'Gone to pick up a **doodah**.'

'I wish he'd said, I wanted a **mackonky** to go with this **shmongah**.'

'I think I've got one of them, over by there by the **whatyoumacallit**. See it?'

'Aye, great stuff. I thought for a moment I'd *afta* borrow one off **Woducall**.'

'He 'asn't got one, he uses a different **do-ins**.'

45

doodah

See **dooberry**.

doolally-pip/doolally-tap

Crazy, weird, loopy.

> **Example:**
> '*Yerd* about Bob?'
> 'No?'
> '*Bin* sectioned he 'as. They locked 'im up in the psychiatric 'ospital.'
> 'Why?'
> 'He went **doolally-tap**, *mun*.'
> 'As good a reason as any, I *spoze*.'

Drive

Generic name for the driver of a public transport vehicle.

> **Example:**
> (commonly heard when the occupants of a double-decker exit at the bus station)
> 'Cheers, **Drive**.'
> 'Cheers, **Drive**.'
> 'Cheers, **Drive**.'
> 'Cheers, **Drive**.'
> 'Cheers, **Drive**.'
> 'Thank you, Driver.' (middle-class passenger), etc.

dunnow

Don't know.

Example:

'*Ooze* this girl *oo* d'keep ringin' *yer* for *ew* and do 'ang up when I d'say *ew en* in?'

'**Dunnow**, love. Must be a wrong number.'

dutty moch

Dirty pig. *Moch* is pronounced as in the Scottish *loch*. Also **dutty mwch**.

Example:

'*Dwn ew* come traipsin' all *thaaaa* muck through the 'ouse! Take *ewer* boots off and leave 'em outside, *ew* **dutty moch**.'

duw duw

Tut tut, would you believe it, eh?

Example:

'Did *ew* go to the match, *butt*?'

'Aye, **duw duw**, *weem* top of the league, they're bottom and they stuffed us!'

'**Duw duw**.'

'**Duw duw** indeed!'

dwn

Don't/doesn't.

Example:

'**Dwn** put that 'ot tea on that new table without a coaster underneath, *ew*'ll mark it.'

'*Wha*?'

'Never mind. Too late. I can't never keep *nuffink* nice in this 'ouse.'

dwt

Tiny, very short. Also **twt**.

> **Example:**
> 'I love *ewer* weddin' *four-tors*, Brenda. Why's the bridesmaid on the left kneelin' down?'
> '*Thaaaa*'s Val. She *en* kneelin' down, *sheez* stood up. *Sheez onny* a little **dwt**.'

E

emptyin' down

Raining heavily, pouring, monsoon conditions.

> **Example:**
> 'Did *ew* remember to give the garden a good waterin'?'
> 'I *oven* 'ad chance yet, love. It's *bin* **emptyin' down** all mornin'. I'll do it *now in a minute* as soon as the rain stops.'

ennew

Aren't you?

> **Example:**
> '**Ennew** pleased Wales beat England today?'
> 'No, I lost money, didn't I?'
> 'Wha', *ew* bet on England to win?'
> 'No, I bet £100 they *wdn* turn up.'

ew

You. Sounds like 'few' without the 'F'.

Example:

'Where's **ew** *gwyin*'?'

'The cricket match. Why? Where's **ew** *gwyin*'?'

'To watch some paint dry.'

'I *tellew wha*', sod the cricket – I think I'd be better off *gwyin*'
with **ew**.'

ewer

Your. Sounds like 'Fewer' without the 'F'.

Example:

'Wha' time's **ewer** bus?'

'Ten to twelve.'

'Well, *ew*'d better get a move on or *youm gwyin*' to miss it.'

...AND AS IT'S WALES, IT'LL BE EMPTYIN' DOWN ALL DAY.

49

F

fart with daps on

Very fast. See **diarrhoea with daps on**.

fell it down

Dropped it.

> **Example:**
> 'I bought a pint at the bar and blinkin' **fell it down** on the way back to our table.'

four-tor

Picture/photograph.

> **Example:**
> '*Ew shouldda* seen Bob fall down comin' out the club *Satdee* night. Classic, *mun*.'
> 'Did *ew* get a **four-tor**?'
> 'No.'
> 'Pity, I'd 'ave paid good money to see *thaaaa*.'

frages

For ages.

> **Example:**
> 'Hiya, *butt*, I *oven* seen *ew* **frages**.'
> 'Aye. I've *bin* away **frages**.'

funedral

Funeral.

Example:
'*Our bamp*'s **funedral**'s next Thursday.'
'*Ew* 'avin' a *buffy*?'
'Aye.'
'*Tidy* – where's it to and wha' time?'

fur coats and no knickers

Ostentatious, pretentious, above one's station.

Example:
'Cor, flippin' 'eck, that family wha' just moved into our street are a bit posh.'
'Posh! Bloody *shoni oi's*, *butt*. Know 'em well. **Fur coats and no knickers**, *mun*.'

G

gallumpin'

Stampeding, moving quickly and recklessly.

Example:
'When *ew* come to bed *afta* me in the night, *willew* try and do it a bit quieter?'
'Why's *thaaaa*, love?'
''Cos *ew* d'sound like a blinkin' 'erd of elephants **gallumpin'** up the stairs. *Ew* d'wake me up every time!'

gambo

Go-cart. Kids made these from old wheels and any old planks of wood they could get their hands on. Also **bwgi**.

gambon

Rustic farmer type. Waxed jacket, corduroy trousers, green wellies, rosy cheeks, rugged looking.

Example:
'What was the Royal Welsh Show like, *butt*?'
'Same as every *yer*, *butt*. Sheep, goats, cows, rabbits, dogs, cats. Nothin' changes.'
'**Gambons**?'
'Swarmin' with 'em.'

gimme-um yer

Pass those to me.

Example:
'I 'ope *ew en* thinkin' of *gutsin'* all them Maltesers on *ewer* own, *arrew*?'
'Well, I was plannin' on it.'
'*Ew*'d better **gimme-um yer** before *ew* d'scoff the lot, *ew gutsy* pig.'

gissit

Give it to me.

Example:
'Where to is the *remort* by?'
'It's by *yer* by me.'

'Well **gissit** *yer*, I wanna put the footy on.'
'Sod off, *ew en* 'avin' no footy on until "Corrie" 'ave finished!'

golloppin'

Swigging, guzzling quickly.

Example:
'I *dunnow* wha's wrong with me. I can't stop *wazzin'* today.'
'I know wha's wrong *withew. Nuffink.* Since *ew* got up this mornin' *ew*'ve *bin* **golloppin'** cups of tea down *ew* faster than someone *oo* 'ave just crawled naked from one end of the Sahara Desert to the other, *like*.'

gompin'

Unattractive, ugly, unappealing,etc. See **boggin'**.

gorra/gorroo

Got to/have to/must.

Example:
'Comin' fishin' with us tomorrow?'
'Can't *butt*, **gorra** take the missus out.'
'Wha'? Takin' the missus out instead of goin' fishin'. *Wossermarrer*?
'**Gorroo**, *mun* – it's our anniversary.'

gorrew

Got you.

Example:
'I **gorrew** a lovely jumper and *ew oven* wore it once yet.'

gozz

Gossip.

Example:

"Ave I got some **gozz** for *ew*!'

'*Wossit* about?'

'Bob's missus.'

'*Yerd* it, *mun*. Old 'at, that is. Come back when *ew*'ve got *summut* new to tell me.'

granch

Affectionate term for one's grandfather. Also **bamp/bampi**.

Example:

'Our **granch** was in the trenches in World War I when the first bullet was fired.'

'Did he live to tell the tale?'

'Ooooh, aye. He was back in C<u>w</u>mcarn when the second one was fired.'

gutsin'

Eating greedily.

Example:

'Where by is Bob to?'

'Last time I seen 'im he was in the canteen **gutsin'** chips like there was no tomorrow.'

gutsy

Greedy or gluttonous.

Example:
'Where's all them doughnuts to?'
'I ate 'em.'
'*Ew* **gutsy** bastard!'

gwli

Back alley, lane.

Example:
'Good mornin', Mrs Bale.'
'Good mornin', Mrs Ramsey.'
'Where's *ewer* Gareth to?'
'Where he always is. *Heez* out the back kickin' a ball up and
down the **gwli** – which will get 'im absolutely nowhere!'
'I know the feelin', *our* Aaron's the same.'

gwnk

An eccentric or odd person. Similar to the 1960s 'beatnik',
used to describe someone who doesn't conform, either because
of their outlook or the way they dress.

Example:
'Have *ew* seen *our* Julie's new boyfriend?
'No.'
'*Heez* one of them goths, *mun*.'
'Goth?'
'Aye. All dressed in black, black 'air, black fingernails, black eye
make-up, black lipstick.'
'Looks like a **gwnk** then.'
'Aye, that's the type.'

gwyin'

Going.

> **Example:**
> 'Where *arrew* **gwyin'**, *butt*?'
> 'I *en* **gwyin'** nowhere, I'm comin' back.'

gwzgogs

Gooseberries.

> **Example:**
> 'If *ew* **dwn** eat them sprouts, *ew en* 'avin' no puddin'.'
> 'Wha's for puddin'?'
> '**Gwzgog** tart.'
> '**Gwzgog** tart! Yuck! Too sour, *mun*. I'd rather eat the sprouts
> and leave the puddin', to be honest.'

gyp

Trouble, difficulty.

> **Example:**
> 'I see *ewer* car's back on the road.'
> 'Aye, but for 'ow long? It went fine for a fortnight and yesterday
> it started givin' me **gyp** again.'

H

'angin'

Probably derived from the Welsh word *angen*, meaning 'need'.
Used when someone's in a hopeless state, e.g. drunk, or a place
is terribly untidy.

> **Example:**
> 'She was **'angin'**, *mun*, really off 'er face!'
> 'Aye, *sheez* like it all the time, *mun*. No wonder 'er 'ouse is
>   **'angin'**.'

'ave a whiff

1. Have a rest. 2. Don't be rash, think before you act.

> **Example:**
> 'Flippin' 'eck, I used to run up this mountain when I was a kid!'
> 'Aye and me – *less* **'ave a whiff** by *yer* for a bit before we d'carry
>   on, *is it?*'

...or

> 'Oi, I *yerd ew*'ve *bin* 'avin' it off with my missus!'
> ''**Ave a whiff**, *butt* – it was *onny* the once.'
> 'Oh, sorry to 'ave bothered *ew*.'

hayputh

1. Miniscule amount, tiny. 2. Idiot, dolt, foolish person.

> **Example:**
> 'Cuppa?'
> 'Yes, please.'
> 'Sugar?'

'Oh, I'm tryin' to cut down – *jest* a **hayputh**, please.'
'What *arrew* cuttin' down for? I've seen more meat on a butcher's pencil.'
'I'm gettin' to look like a right *bomper* lately.'
'*Bomper*! *Ew* look as if *ew* could put on a few pounds to me, *ew* daft **hayputh**.'

'Ow be?

How are you? Also '**Ow do?**

> **Example:**
> "**Ow do**, *butt*?'
> 'Not so bad, *butt* – '**ow be**?

'owlin'

1. Very drunk. 2. Very scruffy, untidy, unkempt.

> **Example:**
> 'Just saw Mary comin' out the pub.'
> 'Was she '**owlin'**?'
> '*Sheez* always '**owlin'**, *mun*, but aye, she was '**owlin'** an all.'

I

in a bit

Soon.

> **Example:**
> "'Ow long's my dinner *gwyin'* to be?'
> 'Just puttin' it in the microwave, love – it'll be ready **in a bit**.'

in a minute

At some indeterminable point in the future. Definitely NOT in a minute's time, and not to be confused with **Now in a minute**.

> **Example:**
> 'When *arrew gwyin'* to do the washin' up?'
> **'In a minute.'**
> '*Ew* said that 'alf hour ago.'
> '*Jest 'ave a whiff, willew* – I *oven* got around to it yet, *mun.*'

inne

Isn't he?

> **Example:**
> 'I saw Dai down the pub earlier. *Heez* drunk all the time, **inne**?'
> **'Inne** *jest.*'

in-orf

In-off (in snooker, billiards, pool).

Commonplace in snooker/billiard halls when I was growing up in the 1960s. Used when the cue ball goes into the pocket off another ball. Whilst the term is actually 'in-off', the older gents always used the very exaggerated 'posh' English version, **in-orf**, to describe the event when it happened. Even with the advent of televised snooker and the commentators referring to it as an 'in-off', my father and people of his generation, even as far as the late 1990s, still referred to **in-orfs** every time it happened.

is it?

Tag question. Used at the end of statements and doesn't really require a response. Probably intended to confirm that a listener has either heard or understood what was said. Also **isn't it?**, **innit?**

> **Example:**
> '*Gwyin*' down the pub *afta*, **is it?**'
> 'Aye, I'll 'ave a couple of pints, **innit?**'
> 'Nice 'ow they've done it up, mind, **innit?**'
> 'Oh, I *en gwyin*' down the Red Lion. I'm *gwyin*' down the King's 'ead, **innit?**'
> 'It's about time they done that up and all, **isn't it?**'
> 'Anyhow, can't 'ang about. *Traaaa.*'
> '*Traaaa.*'

issages

For a long time.

> **Example:**
> 'Hiya, *butt – oven* see *ew* **issages**.'
> 'Aye, *bin* away.'
> 'Anywhere nice?'
> 'HMP Cardiff.'

J

jamine?

Shortened, handy version of the seemingly obligatory phrase, 'D'ya know what I mean?', which people feel compelled to tag on to the end of every sentence.

> **Example:**
> 'I like watchin' rugby on the telly but I *dwn* think I'd be bothered about *gwyin'* to the Principality Stadium to watch it. **Jamine?**'

jest

Just, only.

> **Example:**
> 'So, 'ow many boyfriends 'ave *ew* 'ad before me, then?'
> '**Jest** a few... Bob, George, Tom, Dai, Ron, Pete, another Bob, Phil, Ryan, Tony, Gareth, Paul, Roger, Eric, and the Male Voice Choir.'
> 'Oh, **jest** a few, then.'
> 'Aye. Oh, and the Rugby Club.'

jew

Dew.

> **Example:**
> 'Oh, I love these early mornin's. Runnin' through the meadow with gay abandon. The trees swayin' majestically in the mornin' breeze. The flowers kissed by the mornin' **jew**...'

juke

Duke.

Example:
'Is Prince Charles still the Prince of Wales?'
'Aye. Why's *thaaaa*, *butt*?'
'Bloke on telly last night called 'im the **Juke** of Cornwall.'

K

keiffer

Young, attractive, single females of easy virtue. NB It rhymes with Pfeiffer, as in Michelle Pfeiffer.

Example:
'We 'ad a great night down the club last night, *butt*.'
'Plenty of **keiffer** there?'
'Wall to wall, *butt*. Couldn't fail. Even *ew* would 'ave pulled!'
'Cheeky bastard!'

kilt

Killed.

Example:
'I seen that new film last night.'
'Lemme guess, he died in the end?'
'Aye, well not so much died, *like*. Got **kilt**.'

knackered it up

Broke it.

Example:

'I *bin* and gone and *fallen* our 13th-century Ming vase *down*.'

'Is it still in one piece?'

'No, I've **knackered it up**, *butt*.'

kokum

Sly, crafty, cunning.

Example:

'I can't believe it! Fred 'ave stitched me up again!'

'I *dunnow* why *ew* trust 'im, *butt*. *Heez* a **kokum** bastard.'

koya

Choir.

Example:

'There was a lovely **koya** down the *stute* last night.'

'Can't beat a good male voice, *butt*.'

'Oh aye, I d'come over all *mortional*, *mun*, when I d'listen *twum*.'

L

la butt

Left-handed.

> **Example:**
> 'I *bin* and went and bought 'im a guitar for 'is birthday and *heez* blinkin' **la butt**, *inne*! Spent a king's ransom on that I did, and it *en* no good *twim*.'

lamwidge

Language.

> **Example:**
> 'I thought these job advertisements was supposed to be equal opportunities.'
> 'They are, nobody should be excluded from applyin' for any jobs these days.'
> 'Well, I can't apply for this one – it's all written in the Welsh **lamwidge**, *mun*!'

learn

Teach, instruct.

> **Example:**
> ''Ow did rugby trainin' go tonight, son?'
> '*Tidy*, *mun* – they **learnt** us 'ow to moon outta the back of the bus ready for when we d'go on tour.'
> 'I can't believe wha' they d'**learn** kids these days. When I was playin', things like moonin' outta the bus window used to come natural, *mun*!'

lend

Borrow.

Example:
'Can't I **lend** *ewer* pencil?'
'Aye, I'll 'ave it back tomorrow, no problem.'

lerrew

Let you.

Example:
'I went out with Dolores from the strip club last night.'
'Any luck?'
'*Woddya* mean?
'Did she **lerrew**?
'Well, *less jest* say I <u>wnt</u> be seein' 'er again.'
'*Thaaaa*'s a 'no', then.'

less

Let's.

Example:
'I *tellew wha'*, **less** 'ave another pint, then **less** go 'ome, *is it?*'
'**Less** go now, I reckon, while we can still walk.'

lickle tiny

See **little tiny**.

like

Not used as the English 'like'. A word tagged onto sentences for no real apparent reason. Commonly used throughout Wales and can be interchanged with **look**, which is also used in the same way.

> **Example:**
> '*Weem gwyin*' down the pub *afta*, **like**.'
> 'Wha' time *arrew gwyin*' down, **look**?'
> '*Apparce* seven. *Weem gwyin*' to watch the darts match, **like**.'
> 'I'll come down at *apparce* seven as well, then. I do enjoy a game of darts, **look**.'

little tiny

Very small, minute. Opposite of **big massive**.

lock

Look. Regional variation in the pronunciation of **look**, as used in the context of **like**. See **like**.

> **Example:**
> "Ow *arrew* gettin' on, *butt*?'
> 'I'm *bard*, **lock**.'
> '*Bard*? 'Ow come?'
> '*Bin* overdoin' it, **lock**.'
> 'That's not like *ew*, *butt*. Overworkin', *like*?'
> 'No. Overdrinkin', **lock**.'
> 'Well, *Weem* all guilty of *thaaaa*, *like*.'

look

See **like**.

looksee

Investigate, look up, make reference to.

Example:
'Give us that 'Radio Times' so I can 'ave a **looksee** what's on the telly *afta*.'
'*Dwn* bother *ewer*self luv, there's football on.'
'Aye, well *ew* can forget that, I'll have a **looksee** to what we're actually 'avin' on.'
'In that case, I'll have a **looksee** if they got it on down the club.'

lush

Pleasing to the eye, attractive.

Example:
'Seen Katie's new boyfriend?'
'Phwwoooaaarrr, aye! **Lush**, *inne*!'

M

mackonky

See **dooberry**.

mankin'

Dirty, disgusting, smelly, etc. Also **manky**.

Example:
'Our dog 'ave *bin* and gone and jumped in the river, then rolled in mud *afta*. *Heez* blinkin' **mankin'** he is, aye!'

manky

Alternative to **mankin'**.

Example:
'I seen that tramp *oo* do 'ang around down by the bus station today. *Heez* blinkin' **manky** he is, aye.'

mingin'

Unattractive, ugly, unappealing, etc. See **boggin'**.

mitchin'

Playing truant, skipping school. See **mwtchin'**.

Example:
'Well son, wha' did *ew* learn in school today?'
'**Mitchin**.'

mochyn dee

Dirty pig. Also **mwchyn dee** (alternative pronunciation).

Example:
'Cor, flippin' 'eck – Pete came out the chip shop, fell his pie down on the pavement, picked it up and ate it!'

'*Ychafi*, **mochyn dee**!'
'*Ychafi*, aye. **M**w**chyn dee**!'

moithered

Hot and bothered, flustered. NB Pronounced 'moy-thered'.

Example:
'Them kids 'ave *bin* playin' up all day and I *oven* got 'alf the
 things done that I wanted to do.'
"Ow *arrew* now, love?'
'**Moithered**!'

mortional

Emotional.

Example:
'Wha' was it like bumpin' into *ewer* ex *lie-gaaaa* after so many
 yers?'
'I found it a very **mortional** experience. I still 'ate the bastard,
 though!'

mucker

Generic name for an acquaintance. Similar to 'mate', 'buddy',
etc.

Example:
''*Ow be*, **mucker**?'
'*Tidy*, *butt*, and *ew* too?'

mulin'

1. Unattractive, ugly, unappealing,etc. See **boggin'**.
2. Good hiding (in the violent sense).

> **Example:**
> 'Scrap down the club last night.'
> 'What 'appened?'
> 'Someone told Norman he was **mulin'**, so he took 'im outside
>   and give 'im a good **mulin'**.'
> 'Done a *tidy* job, did he?'
> 'Oh aye. Knocked *seven bells* out of 'im.'

mun

Similar to the US 'man'. Added to a sentence for emphasis,
to create a feeling of urgency, or as a term of endearment, for
both sexes.

> **Example:**
> 'C'mon *mun*!'
> '*Wossermarrer*?'
> 'If *ew dwn* put a move on *weem gwyin'* to miss the kick off.'
> 'Keep a cool 'ead, **mun**. Plenty of time yet.'

muntin'

Unattractive, ugly, unappealing, etc. See **boggin'**.

mwchyn

Pig. See **mochyn dee**.

m<u>w</u>ci nic

Mischief.

> **Example:**
> 'I see Mrs Evans 'ave *bin* 'avin' trouble with 'er son again. Sent home from school today he was.'
> 'Not surprised, *heez* full of **m<u>w</u>ci nic**.'

m<u>w</u>sh

Generic name for an acquaintance. Similar to 'mate', 'buddy', etc.

> **Example:**
> 'Hiya, *bim*. 'Ows it *gwyin*?'
> 'Not so bad, **m<u>w</u>sh** – 'ow's *ewer*self?'

m<u>w</u>tchin'

Playing truant, skipping school. Also **mitchin'**.

> **Example:**
> '*Woddya* mean *ew*'ve never *yerd* of Winston Churchill? *Heez* blinkin' famous, *mun*. Didn't *ew* go to school?'
> 'Must've *bin* **m<u>w</u>tchin** the day we done 'im.'

N

nesh

Lightweight, namby-pamby.

Example:

'I've got a T-shirt and shorts on, *ew*'ve got a T-shirt and shorts on, and look at Bob. *Wassermarrer* with 'im, *mun*? *Heez* got jeans, a T-shirt, pullover and a coat on. He reckons *heez* cold!'

'*Heez* always the same, 'im. Bloody **nesh** he is, *mun*.'

nobblin'

Extremely cold.

Example:

'What was the Christmas Day swim at Tenby like this *yer*?'

'Didn't go, *butt*, it was **nobblin'**. I didn't even set foot out of the door all day.'

'*Dwn* blame *ew*, *butt*. I can't understand why they d'do it.'

'They d'do it because *theym* mental, *mun*. *Thaaaa*'s why they d'do it!'

now afta

Sometime in the future.

Example:

'*Ew* comin' down the club with us now?'

'No, I got a few things to do first. I'll see *ew* **now afta**.'

now in a minute

Sometime later. Certainly not soon.

Example:

'*Willew* turn *thaaaa* football off? I want to watch "Casualty".'
'I'll turn it off **now in a minute**, love, when it finishes.'
"'Ow long is left?'
'They're three minutes into the first 'alf.'

now just

Immediately, straight away.

Example:

'*Weem gwyin*' to be late if you *dwn* 'urry up. 'Ow long *arrew gwyin*' to be?'
'I'm just puttin' my coat on. I'll be there **now just**.'

nowt

Nothing.

Example:

'Will the prisoner in the dock please stand. Do you have anything to say before I pass sentence?'
'**Nowt**.'
'Fair enough, ten years. Take him down.'

nuffink

Nothing.

Example:

'Wha's the *gozz*?'
'**Nuffink** to report, *butt*. It's all quiet at the moment.'

nupps

No.

> **Example:**
> 'Fancy a cuppa, *butt*?'
> '*Ew* know me, I never say **nupps** to a cuppa.'

O

of

Have.

> **Example:**
> '*Ew* shouldn't **of** done *thaaaa*.'

old 'at

Out of date, old news.

> **Example:**
> '*Waaassssaaaaaa* CD *ew* got by there, *butt*?'
> 'The Manics' new album.'
> '*Less* 'ave a look. That *en* their new album. *Bin* out *yers* that 'as,
> *mun*. **Old 'at** that is. They've 'ad four out since *thaaaa*.'

onny

Only.

> **Example:**
> '*Arrew* sure *youm* alright to drive?'
> 'Aye, I've **onny** 'ad 16 pints.'
> '*Tidy*, *less* go.'

oo

Who.

Example:
'The bus was late on *Satdee* and by the time I got 'ome, I missed 'alf of "Doctor **Oo**".'

oojackapivvy

See **dooberry**.

ool

Whole.

Example:
'Remember that day Wales got beat by Western Samoa?'
'Aye, it was a good job we didn't play the **ool** of it!'

oolmeal

Wholemeal.

Example:
"'Ow's *ewer* diet *gwyin'*?'
'Alright, *butt*. I do 'ave that **oolmeal** bread now for my
    samwidges.'
'*Tidy*. Wha' did *ew* 'ave in 'em today?'
'Chips and tomato sauce. Lovely, *mun*.'
'Lost any weight?'
'Not really, *butt*. Put a few pounds on if anythin', *like*.'

oolsome

Wholesome, nicey nicey, sincere.

Example:
'I see *ew*'ve stopped botherin' with Colleen, then?'

'Aye, two faced, *mun*. Nice enough to *ewer* face but d'slag *ew* off behind *ewer* back.'

'I always thought she was too sweet to be **oolsome**.'

oove

Who has.

Example:
'**Oove** moved *thaaaa remort* from by the side of the telly?

'Me. I moved it from over by there to over by *yer*.'

'Why?'

''Cos it's easier for me to reach when it's over by *yer* than over by there.'

ooze

1. Whose. 2. Who's. 3. Hose.

Example:
'**Ooze ooze** is *thaaaa*?'

'Mine, wanna *lend* it?'

'Aye. I wanna give the *bailey* a good **ooze** down. Covered in bloody dog *pwp*, *mun*.'

'Dirty bastards. **Ooze** *bin* lettin' their dog *cack* all over *ewer bailey*?'

'Us.'

'Oh.'

ort

Hotel. Shortened 'affectionate' name for a pub named 'The ... Hotel'.

Example:
'Where was *ew* last night? I said I'd meet *ew* in the **Ort**.'
'Well, I went to the Cwmcarn **Ort** and *ew* wasn't there. Then I went to the Crosskeys **Ort** and *ew* wasn't in there either.'
'Bugger. I was in the Newbridge **Ort**.'
'Typical, went to the wrong **Ort**.'

our...

Precedes any reference to a member of one's family or possession.

Example:
'Just *bin* round **our** 'ouse. There *en* nobody there. Where's everybody to?'
'**Our** mam, **our** dad and **our** Julie 'ave gone down the 'ospital with **our** Dai.'
'*Wassermarrer?*'
'**Our** Bob *fell* a shovel *down* on 'is foot and *knackered it up*.'

oven

Haven't.

Example:
'**Oven** *ew* cooked dinner yet?'
'No, I **oven**.'
'Why not? *Ew bin* 'ome *frages*.'
'I **oven** *bin* able to light the oven.'

P

pelanty

A penalty. A period of free play unchallenged by opponents or a shot at goal following an infringement in rugby and football. **Pelanty** is frequently used in place of 'penalty' by Welsh pundits during the half-time and post-match summing-up on televised rugby and football matches.

pervin'

Letching, leering, having impure thoughts.

> **Example:**
> 'Unless **pervin'** is somethin' *ew* can put on a CV, *ewers* is *gwyin'* to be pretty blank.'
> 'Thanks, *Bryn*.'

pitcher

Picture/photograph. Also **four-tor**.

> **Example:**
> 'Alright, *Bryn*? Fancy poppin' round our 'ouse to 'ave a look at our 'oliday **pitchers**?'
> 'Not if *theym* as bad as the *four-tors ew* took last *yer*, *butt*.'

potch

Builders' term for an awkward/fiddly job.

> **Example:**
> 'I'll build extensions, install new kitchens, sweet as a nut – but I'm not interested in any **potch** jobs.'

potchin'

Messing about (in the extra-marital sense).

> **Example:**
> '*Yerd* about Ron?'
> 'No.'
> 'His missus caught 'im **potchin'** with that tart *oo* d'work down
> the chip shop.'

Q
Q

The only audible remnant from the term 'Thank you' when
uttered, usually, by people in the retail/pub trade.

> **Example:**
> 'I'll 'ave seven pints of bitter, three Guinnesses, four whiskeys,
> two vodka and cokes, three packets of cheese and onion, a
> bag of nuts and a steak and kidney pie – one minute in the
> microwave with brown sauce. Oh, and 'ave one *ewer*self love.'
> '**Q**.'

R

rampin'

Very painful.

> **Example:**
> 'I see *youm* back on *ewer* feet since *ew bust ewer* leg. 'Ow is it?'
> 'Now and again it d'give me *gyp*.'

'In wha' way?'
'Well, it was fine all day yesterday, but the day before it was
    bloody **rampin'**!'

reckin'

Complaining, grumbling.

Example:
'*Bin* in that new pub what 'ave just opened in town?'
'No. Everybody that 'ave *bin* in there 'ave *bin* **reckin'** about the
    price of the beer in there.'

remort

TV remote control.

Example:
'I've searched this 'ouse and I can't find the **remort** anywhere.'
'I *speckt* it's down the back of the settee with all the other *do-ins*
    that d'slip down there.'

Rodney

Scruffy bloke.

Example:
'Did *ew* go to the weddin'?'
'Aye. *Ew shouldda* seen the state of Bob, bearin' in mind it
    was a weddin' and *youm* supposed to make an effort, *like*.
    Unwashed 'air, filthy shoes, shirt not ironed, muck all over 'is
    suit. Disgustin', *mun*.'
'Oh, typical of Bob – *heez* a proper **Rodney**, *mun*.'

rowal

Bisyllabic Valleys version of the English 'roll'.

Example:
'Can I 'ave an 'am **rowal** please?'

'Certainly, sir. Would *ew* like tomato?'

'No, that would be an 'am and tomato **rowal** – it's an 'am **rowal** I want. *Jest* a **rowal** with some butter with 'am in it, please. *Jest* a plain 'am **rowal**.'

'Oh right, I see what *ew* mean, I'll make it *now just*. White or brown **rowal**?'

'Brown, please.'

'Lettuce?'

S

Saaarpnin?

(always a question) A form of greeting. Alternative to, 'ello', 'alright, butt', etc. An amalgamation of the words 'What's happening?'

> **Example:**
> '**Saaarpnin**, *butt*?'
> 'Nothin' much. **Saaarpnin** *withew*?'
> 'Same as *ew, butt*. Nothin'.'

scraggy

Thin, pale, emaciated.

> **Example:**
> '*Thaaaa*'s Ron's new girlfriend over by there, look.'
> 'Which one, the smart one with the blue top on?'
> 'No, the **scraggy** one with 'er.'
> 'Bloody 'ell, is that an _wman_? It d'look more like a whippet with a Donald Trump wig on.'

scram

1. A scratch from a cat or any other beast with claws.
2. To scratch.

> **Example:**
> 'Is that a **scram** mark on *ewer* arm?'
> 'Aye. I picked Bob's cat up, and he **scrammed** me all the way down.'

scruntin'

Unattractive, ugly, unappealing,etc. See **boggin'**.

Sdim ots

Am I bothered?

> **Example:**
> 'I *yerd* Tom 'ave found out *ew*'ve *bin potchin'* with 'is missus.'
> '**Sdim ots**. Occupational 'azard, *butt*.'

seven bells

Unit used to measure the severity of a beating that one has received.

> **Example:**
> ''Ow did the boxin' go?'
> 'Not bad.'
> 'Did *thaaaa* local boy win 'is bout?
> 'No, he 'ad **seven bells** knocked out of 'im.'

shmongah

See **dooberry**.

shoni oi

Scoundrel/rascal. Akin to the contemporary term 'chav'. Also **sh<u>w</u>ni**.

> **Example:**
> 'And *d<u>w</u>n* go fetchin' 'im back to this 'ouse. *Heez* a blinkin' **shoni oi** – and the rest of 'is family.'

shonky

Low quality.

> **Example:**
> 'I bought a pack of 1000 cigarette lighters from the 99p shop.
>   I've tried 37 so far and none of 'em work!'
> '*Arrew* surprised? Everythin' they sell's bloody **shonky**, *mun*.'

shouldda

Should have. Also **should of**.

> **Example:**
> 'I **shouldda** read them instructions before I started messin'
>   about with *thaaa*.'
> '*Whysaaaa*, *butt*?'
> ''Cos I've *bin* and gone and blinkin' *busted* it now.'
> '*Ew* **should of**, *butt*.'

shut tap

The bar is now closed.

> **Example:**
> 'I just *bin* to the bar and it's **shut tap**!'
> 'Didn't *ew yer* the bell for last orders?'
> 'No.'
> 'I did and luckily enough I managed to get 16 pints in.'
> 'Gimme a couple?'
> 'Sod off!'

sh<u>w</u>mae

Hello.

Example:
'**Sh<u>w</u>mae**, Paul.'
'**Sh<u>w</u>mae**, Bob.'
'**Sh<u>w</u>mae**, Dai.'
'**Sh<u>w</u>mae**, Gareth.'
'**Sh<u>w</u>mae**, Pete.'

sh<u>w</u>mai dap

Term used to refer to gaudy things that babies are dressed in.

Example:
"'Ave *ew* seen their baby? It's always **shwmai dap** in *muntin'* pink crocheted stuff – looks like my Nan's loo roll cover!'

spag

An action made by a cat with his/her paw in attack mode. Usually with extended claws.

Example:
'I'm not *gwyin'* round their 'ouse again.'
'Why not? *Theym* a nice couple.'
'*Theym* nice, aye, but I d'get fed up with their cat **spaggin'** me every time they *en* lookin'.'

speckt

Expect.

Example:
'I **speckt** *youm gwyin'* down the club tonight.'
'Aye, but I'll be late, I **speckt**. I'll see *ew now after*.'

spoze

Suppose.

> **Example:**
> 'I **spoze** *ew*'ll be *gwyin'* to the club to watch the football and comin' 'ome drunk, as usual.'
> '*Ew* **spozed** right.'

squit out

Betray, let down.

> **Example:**
> 'We booked a minibus to take us to the match and the boys from the rugby club made their own way. Me and Will 'ad to pay for the *ool* bus between us two!'
> '*Ew shouldda* known the rugby boys would **squit out**, *butt*. They always do.'

squits (the)

Diarrhoea.

> **Example:**
> 'I <u>wnt</u> be *gwyin'* down the club *afta*. I'm 'avin' a night in, *butt*.'
> 'Becomin' a recluse, *arrew*?'
> 'No, I got **the squits**, *mun*.'
> 'Stay where *ew* are, *butt*.'

squitter

Turncoat, traitor.

> **Example:**
> 'After reading your CV and noticing you are known as '**Squitter**

Jenkins', I'm afraid your application to join the Welsh Guards has been turned down.'

starvin'

Cold, wet, windswept.

Example:
'*Ew shouldn't of* come out in this weather, it's blinkin' *tampin'* down. *Youm* soaked through. Quick, come in and I'll get *ew* a towel – take *thaaaa* coat off, it's soakin'. *Ew* look bloody **starvin'**, *mun*.'

stink <u>w</u>ppin'

Reek, smell very badly, pong.

Example:
'Cor, flippin' 'eck. I bumped into that tramp *oo* do 'ang around down the bus station. He d'blinkin' **stink <u>w</u>ppin**, aye.'

stute

Shortened 'affectionate' name for the village Miners' Institute.

Example:
'There's a good band in the **stute** on *Satdee*. *G<u>wy</u>in*'?'
'Which one, Blackwood **stute** or Newbridge **stute**?'
'Both of 'em.'

summut

Something.

Example:

'I 'ope *ew* got me **summut** nice for Christmas.'

'Well I 'ave got *ew* **summut**, aye. Whether it's nice or not is another matter.'

'As long as *ew*'ve kept the receipt, I can change it for **summut** else, I *spoze*.'

swillin'

Drinking heavily.

Example:

'Wha' time's kick-off?'

'Three o'clock.'

'Wha' time's the club open?'

'*Apparce* eight.'

'In the night?'

'In the mornin', *ew* dozy *twonk*.'

'*Tidy*, we can 'ave a few hours' **swillin'** before the game d'start.'

T

taint

It's not. Handy, lazy version of the non-standard English 'it ain't'. Also **tent**.

Example:

'*Ooze* dog's *thaaaa*? It just *pwped* on the pavement.'

'**Taint** mine – not any more, anyway. I *ent* pickin' that lot up and takin' it 'ome.'

tampin'

1. Really angry.   2. Raining very heavily.
3. Bouncing/bumping.

Example:
'I'm blinkin' **tampin'** I am, aye. It's *bin* **tampin'** down all day
   and them kids 'ave *bin* **tampin'** their ball against our fence all
   bloody afternoon.'
'No wonder *youm* **tampin'**.'

tapped

Odd, eccentric.

Example:
'Derek got banned from drivin' for ten years last Friday, and
   yesterdee he went out and bought a new car!'
'*Nowt* would surprise me about 'im – bloody **tapped** he is.

Tellew wha'

Hey, listen to this!

Example:
'**Tellew wha'**, *sheez* a bit of a looker, 'er over there by the bar.'
'*Ew* wanna curb *ewer* drinkin', *butt*, thaaaaa's *ewer* mother!'

tent

It's not. Handy, lazy version of the already non-standard **it ent**.

Example:
'**Tent** easy to give up smokin'.'
'It is. I've give it up 'undreds of times!'

thaaaa

That.

> **Example:**
> 'Give us **thaaa** by there.'
> 'Wha'?'
> '**Thaaa** by there, by your foot.'
> 'This?'
> 'Aye, *bung* it over *yer*, *willew*.'

there's loveleeee

Expression of joy.

> **Example:**
> 'Hello June, fancy bumpin' into *ew* by *yer*. **There's loveleeee** to see *ew*.'
> '**There's loveleeee** to see *ew* too. Wha's the *gozz*?'
> 'I'm a grandmother now. *Our* Mercedes 'ave 'ad a little 'un.'
> 'Aw, **there's loveleeee**. Boy or girl?'
> 'Boy. Seven pound four. 'Is name's Benedict *afta* Sherlock 'Olmes. *Yer's* a *pitcher* of 'im.'
> 'Awwww, **there's loveleeee**. Nice name too.'

theym

They are.

> **Example:**
> 'Look at that lot, it's *tampin'* down with rain and **theym** stood around outside as if *nuffink's* 'appenin'!'
> '**Theym** mental, *mun*, always 'ave *bin*.'

tidy

A real monster. **Tidy** can mean just about anything positive, pleasurable, good, neat, smart, satisfying, etc., that the user chooses. The list of possible definitions is inexhaustible, but here are a few ideas.

> **Example:**
> "Ow's it *gwyin'*, *butt*?'
> '**Tidy**, *mun*, aye.'
> "Ow did the interview go?'
> '**Tidy**, *butt* – I got the job. They gimme a maths test and I done it **tidy** by all accounts.'
> '**Tidy**! Much different to what *ew*'ve *bin* doin'?'
> 'Oh aye, **tidy** job this is. *Gorra* dress **tidy** and all.'
> '**Tidy**. Office job, is it?'
> 'Aye. *Gorra* get some **tidy** shoes before I start. I've got a **tidy** suit and **tidy** shirts, but my shoes *en* up to much.'
> 'Well *ew gorra* create a **tidy** impression.'
> 'Well, I *gorra* tidy my 'ouse before I get into town for them shoes.'
> 'All the best, *butt*. See *ew in a bit*, I *spoze*. I'll tell my missus about *ewer* new job.'
> '**Tidy**. See *ew*, *butt*.'

toffee recs

Extremely poor, low quality. As in the English adjective 'Mickey Mouse', for something that's severely below par.

> **Example:**
> '*Weem* 'avin' a new kitchen. I was thinkin' of tryin' *thaaaa* new buildin' company tha's just opened up in town.'
> 'I _wdn_ bother, *butt*. I've *yerd theym* a **toffee recs** outfit.'

traaaa

Goodbye, farewell, ta-ta.

> **Example:**
> 'OK, **traaaa** – see *ew Sundee*.'
> 'Aye, see *ew Sundee* – **traaaa**.'
> '**Traaaa**.'
> '**Traaaa**.'
> 'Bob, say **traaaa** *twum*.'
> '**Traaaa**.'
> 'Good boy.'

twer

To her – feminine of **twim**.

twernt

It wasn't. Almost certainly a shortened version of the non-standard English phrase 'it weren't'. Also **twozn** (from 'it wasn't').

> **Example:**
> '*Ew* just farted?
> '**Twernt** me.'
> '*Woddya* mean, **twozn** *ew*. There's *onny* us two in *yer* and **twozn** me!'
> 'Oh, in that case, guilty as charged.'

twim

To him – masculine of **twer**.

twonk

Twit, idiot, fool, twpsin… you know the type.

Example:

'Every time we do 'ave faggots for dinner, the 'ouse fuses d'blow out.'

'*Thaaaa*'s 'cos *ew* d'put 'em in the microwave in the foil tray, *ew* **twonk**!'

twp/twpped/twpsin

Stupid.

Example:

'*Yerd* about Bob?'

'No, *wossee* done now?'

'*Heez bin* and gone and bet Dai five grand that within ten years, Newport County will win the FA Cup, the Premiership and the Champions League!'

'*Heez* bloody **twp**, *mun*!'

twt

Very small, tiny (usually as in a child). Also **dwt**.

Example:

''Ow come *ew* d'live in Cardiff and *ew* d'support Man Utd?'

'Dunno, *butt* – I've supported 'em since I was a **twt**.'

twtti down

Crouch, squat, bend.

Example:

'Quick! Come by *yer*. Them girls over by the lake are gettin' undressed to go swimmin'.'

'Can *ew* see anythin'?'

'Aye, but *ew* better **twtti down** by *yer*, otherwise they'll catch us gawpin' at 'em.'

twum

To them.

Example:

'Are we sendin' an invitation **twum**, or not?'

'*Dwn* bother, they never invited us to their dad's *funedral*.'

94

U

up and downer

Confrontation, row.

Example:
'Wassermarrer withew?'
'Oh, I 'ad an **up and downer** with the boss in work again. *Sheez* a bitch.'
'Wosshee like, then?'
'She d'keep *specktin'* me to do *summut.'*
'Unreasonable cow.'

uzbun

Husband.

Example:
'Arrew 'ittin' on me? Wait till I tell my **uzbun**!'
'Go and tell 'im now, love. *Heez* in bed with my missus at the moment.'

V W

warrirriz, right

What it is, right. In telecommunications, the caller's opening gambit, preceding the reason for the call or even who's calling.

Example:
'Hello, British Gas. How can I help?'
'Warrirriz, right, we've *bin* 'avin' trouble with our boiler.'

wass

Originally boy or servant, but now used as a 'tag' when greeting someone without using their name. Similar to the Scouse 'wack' or 'wacker', or the US 'dude' or 'man.'

Example:
'Alright, **wass** – 'ows it *gwyin*?'

wazz

1. Urine. 2. To pee.

Example:
'If this bus *dwn* 'urry up and pull into the bus station. I'm *gwyin'* to **wazz** my kecks.'
'I told *ew* to 'ave a **wazz** before we got on, *mun*.'

wdn

Wouldn't. Sounds like 'wooden' without the 'w'.

Example:
'I **wdn** stick *ewer* finger in that cage, *butt*.'
'Aaaarrrgghhh!'
'Told *ew*. Ew **wdn** listen, would *ew*?'

weem

We are.

Example:
'**Weem** *gwyin'* to Cardiff shoppin' *Satdee*.'
'Oh, **weem** *gwyin'* to Newport.'
'Fancy comin' to Cardiff with us instead?'
'No, **weem** meetin' my sister in Newport *afta*.'

whatewmcallit

See **dooberry**.

Where to is it by?/Where by is it to?

(interchangeable) Where is it?

> **Example:**
> "Ave *ew* seen the *remort*?'
> 'Aye.'
> **'Where to is it by?'**
> 'On the arm of the chair by *yer*. 'Ave *ew* seen the paper?'
> 'Aye.'
> **'Where by is it to?'**
> 'Down by the side of the settee.'

whysaaaa?

Why's that?

> **Example:**
> **'Whysaaaa** by there?'
> **'Whysaaaa?'**
> "Cos it *dwn* belong by there, do it?'
> 'It d'belong where I d'decide to leave it.'

willew

Will you?

> **Example:**
> 'I know *ew* think I'm *reckin'* at *ew* all the time, but tidy *ewer* room
> up **willew**, it's like a *cowin'* tip in there.'

withew

With you.

Example:
'Where *ew* off, *butt*?'
'Off for a meal to celebrate our anniversary.'
'Why *en ewer* missus **withew**?'
'*Sheez gwyin*' to a different restaurant to celebrate it.'

wman

Woman.

Example:
'This is a customer announcement. Will the **wman** *oo* tied 'er child and dog to the trolley shelter please contact the Customer Services desk immediately. RSPCA, NSPCC and Social Services waitin'.'

wnt

Will not or won't.

Example:
'*Arrew gwyin*' abroad this *yer*?'
'Not after last yer. We spent so much money in Benidorm, Fred **wnt** fork out the money.'

woddya

What do you?

Example:
'*Ew* never take me anywhere expensive these days.'
'Get *yer* coat.'

'**Woddya** mean? Where are we *gwyin*?'
'The petrol station.'

wodewcall

See **dooberry**.

woh-vu

What have you?

> **Example:**
> '**Woh-vu** got, *butt*?'
> 'The doctor said I got the flu.'
> '*Bard*?'
> '*Terrible bard, butt*.'

wossat

What is that?

> **Example:**
> '**Wossat** pokin' out from under the settee?'
> 'It's the *remort*. I *bin* lookin' for that.'

wossee

What has he?/What is he?

> **Example:**
> '**Wossee** doin' under the table?'
> 'Lookin' for *summut*.'
> '**Wossee** lost?'
> 'I *dunnow*, *woh-vu* lost, *butt*?'
> 'My *wossnim*.'

Wossermarrer?

What's the matter?

> **Example:**
> '**Wossermarrer** *withew*?'
> '*Ew*! *Thaaaa*'s **wossermarrer** with me!'
> 'I'm sorry I *ast* now.'

wossiss

What is this?

> **Example:**
> '**Wossiss** on the telly?'
> 'A film, *innit*.'

wossit

What is it?

> **Example:**
> '**Wossit** called?'
> '*Oven* got a clue. I *en* really watchin' it to be honest.'

wosshee

Feminine of **wossee**.

wossnim

See **dooberry**.

wozn

Wasn't.

Example:

'I **wozn** *specktin' ew* to get me anythin' for my birthday this *yer*.'
'*Wha'*! After last *yer* when I didn't get *ew* anythin'? *Youm* 'avin' a laugh.'

XYZ

ychafi!

Eurrgghh! Gross! NB Pronounced 'ucher vee', with the ch as in 'loch'.

Example:

'I got 'ome from the shop and someone's dog 'ad taken a dump on the doorstep. I trod in it and walked it right through the 'ouse!'
'Arrgghh, **ychafi**!'

yer

Very versatile interchangeable word for 'ear', 'year', 'here' and 'hear'.

Example:

(at the hospital)
'What *arrew* doin' **yer**?' (here)
'Got *summut* wrong with my **yer**.' (ear)
'*Wha'*? *Ew* mean *ew* can't **yer**?' (hear)
'Aye, *onny* now they've got round to seein' me, but I've 'ad the problem over a **yer**.' (year)

yerd

Past tense of **yer** (heard).

> **Example:**
> '*Avew* **yerd** the new AC/DC album? I played it all day today. Brilliant, aye.'
> 'Aye, I **yerd** it. All the neighbours **yerd** it too. It is good, fair play.'

yesterdee

Yesterday. See **dee**.

yonk

Idiot.

> **Example:**
> '*Dwn* tell me *ew* sent 'im down the road for fags for *ew*. God knows what he'll come back with, probably a pork pie or *summut lie-gaaaa*, I *speckt*. *Heez* a blinkin' **yonk**, *mun*.'

youm

You are. Also **ewm**.

> **Example:**
> 'Where *ew* off to, *butt*?'
> 'Down the bookies. I'm puttin' a fiver on Newport County to win the FA Cup.'
> 'Wha'? **Youm** blinkin' *twp ew* are, *mun*! If *ew* wanna chuck *ewer* money away, *bung* it over by *yer*.'

Just one more thing:
Malapropisms and other bloopers

Malapropism: the mistaken use of a word in place of a similar-sounding one, often with an amusing effect (e.g. 'dance a flamingo' instead of 'flamenco').

Malapropisms are very, very popular in Wales. By definition, they can appear in conversations erroneously at any time and there's no limit to the number of wrong words that can be slipped into a sentence. We're also very fond of just getting things wrong. You know, nearly right, kind of makes sense but definitely wrong. We can't cater for those here – you don't know when they'll crop up – but you should be prepared for them. Even now, after reading and inwardly digesting all the tips in this book, and with your vocabulary expanded to encompass everything in the Phrasebook, you can still fall flat on your face at the hand of a random malapropism or a total misreporting of something which appears to be in context. So, beware and be on the lookout for these, and try to be flexible enough to decipher what the speaker meant to say, had they not included these beauties. Here are a few to set the scene, just to let you know what you may be faced with. After having got this far and as you're now 'fluent' in Valleys-speak, I have deemed it unnecessary to provide translations for these.

Examples:

'It's immortal the way people are treated in hospitals these days.'

'Look at that greyhound! I know they're supposed to be thin, but not that thin, surely. That one looks blinkin' emancipated, mun.'

'You're very talented with numbers. You should go on *Countdown*.'
'I'd be great on there on the numbers section. The letters would be my problem. I'm no good at them mammograms.'

'Do you like Gordon Zola?'
'Italian. Played for Chelsea. Yeah, good player.'
'Well, it is Italian. But it's cheese, you dickhead.'

'When we got the figures in, we plotted them on a graph and it was plain to see that the pigs and troughs reflected the trends that we expected and were typical for that particular data set.'

'When you say you sorted them, do you mean chronologically, numerically or alphabetically?'
'Sorted alphabetically according to size.'

'This three-piece suite you're getting on Saturday – are you having a three-seater, two-seater and a chair, or a three-seater and two chairs? You can get different combinations, you know.'
'Jacket, trousers and waistcoat.'

'This is a classic "chicken and egg" situation.'
'What's a "chicken and egg" situation?'
'Don't put them all in the same basket.'

'This situation in steel is worse than everybody thinks. OK, so they make all the steelworkers repugnant, but what about the other industries dependent on the steel industry? That'll hit the community for six, 'cos they'll go as well!'

'He's just bought a new guitar. Cost him a fortune. Stratter, er… stratter… um, oh, it's a stratter-something anyway.'
'Strattervarious?'
'Might be. Hang on, isn't that a violin?'

'How's your Julie getting on?'
'Very well. Soliciting at the moment.'
'Excellent. What she wanted?'
'Oh aye, she joined a firm of solicitors and within four months they made her a partner.'

'It was right there, so we're told, that Drake was playing bowls when the Spanish Emeralda was first spotted.'

'Well, halfway through the season and still no points. We look a cert for regulation the way things are going.'

'Peter's been accepted at college to study music.'
'Which particular area?'
'Drums and concussion.'

'Can you pick me up a Mars Bar from the venting machine on your way back, please?'

'We've been having some funny phone calls lately so we've gone hysterectomy.'

'There's an excellent brassière opened in town. Good food, good service and cheap. Well worth a try, I've heard.'

'My favourite anthem out of the six nations teams isn't ours, it's the French one.'
'The French one?'
'Aye. *I'll be there, I'll be there. I'll be there, I'll be there, When the coal comes from the Rhondda on that little railroad track, With my little pick and shovel I'll be there.*'
'That doesn't ring a bell with me at all, butt. I'm not sure you've got that right.'

'We've got a PowerPoint presentation this afternoon.'
'Who's felicitating?'
'Kevin. He's about the best we've got at it.'

'You missed it. Anthony got stuck in the revolutionary doors in the foyer. They had to get the engineers to get him out. Bloody hysterical it was, aye.'

'You should have seen the darts team when they won the final last night. Over the moon they were. They were doing handcarts down the street.'

'Pass me that strainer thing out of the cupboard.'
'What thing?
'That sieve thing – you know, for straining the peas.'
'Calendar.'
'Close enough. Yes, that's it. Pass it here, please?'

'We appear to have lost Brian again.'
'Probably pervin' in the lingery department, knowing him.'

'I hit the ball with all the venison I could muster.'

'Hell hath no fury like a woman spermed.'

'Have a listen to this CD. It's a copulation album of rock anthems.'

'His father was born in Cardiff, so he was illegible to play for Wales.'

'You three are a right pair if ever I saw one.'

'It's about time they put their foot down with a firm hand.'

...and my all-time favourite:

'Allegations have been made that I have had my fingers in the till; allegations have been made that I've been fiddling the tote; allegations have been made that I've been drinking the stock. If I find out who the alligator is, there'll be murder!'

Conclusion

Well, that's it really. You now know as much as I do. All you have to do now is try it out. I'm confident that as a visitor you can stride into a restaurant, corner shop, garage, chip shop or village hall and converse, with confidence, with any local you care to approach. Feel free to book your holidays in Wales. Accept any wedding invitations with confidence, safe in the knowledge that even though you may be in deepest Aber-cwm-scwt you'll be more than ready to engage with all the guests, the vicar, the reception gatecrashers – you may even be invited to join in with the scrap in the car park at the end of the night.

Don't be afraid to stop anywhere and ask for directions, but keep the book in your glove compartment just in case. I can't guarantee I'll be the person you stop to ask for guidance to your destination, but I'll do my best.

Acknowledgements

To all people who have, over the years, studied and brought our version of English to the fore, especially John Edwards.

A big thank you to all these contributors, who provided me with many of the quotes seen in the phrasebook: Matt Bale, Clare Billet, Helen Crimmins, Ashley Croome, Joan Clutterbuck, Rose Davies, Ryan Hancocks, Alison Kindred, Robert Lewis, Caroline Marks, Sallie Mogford, Jo Naylor, Rory O'Donnell, Ian Prosser, Katie Smith, Owain Thomas.

...and to Robert Lewis's book on Wenglish: *The Dialect of the South Wales Valleys* (second edition), published by Y Lolfa in 2016.

Also by the author:

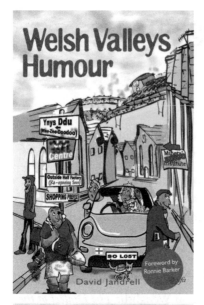

£3.95

£3.95

£3.95

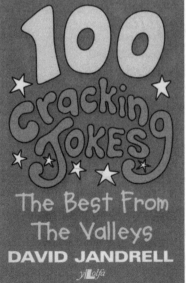

£3.95

Welsh Valleys Phrasebook is just one of a whole range of publications from Y Lolfa. For a full list of books currently in print, send now for your free copy of our new full-colour catalogue. Or simply surf into our website

www.ylolfa.com

for secure on-line ordering.

TALYBONT CEREDIGION CYMRU SY24 5HE
e-mail ylolfa@ylolfa.com
website www.ylolfa.com
phone (01970) 832 304
fax 832 782

Ask for a print quote!
01970 832 304